Published by Red Panda, an imprint of Westland Books, a division of Nasadiya Technologies Private Limited, in 2025

No. 269/2B, First Floor, 'Irai Arul', Vimalraj Street, Nethaji Nagar, Alapakkam Main Road, Maduravoyal, Chennai 600095

Westland, the Westland logo, Red Panda and the Red Panda logo are the trademarks of Nasadiya Technologies Private Limited, or its affiliates.

Copyright © Nasadiya Technologies Private Limited, 2025

ISBN: 9789371971409

10 9 8 7 6 5 4 3 2 1

All rights reserved

Images sourced from Freepik & Vecteezy

Designed by Karthik K.

Printed at Nutech Print Services Pvt. Ltd

No part of this book may be reproduced, or stored in a retrieval system, or transmitted in any form or by any means, electronic, mechanical, photocopying, recording, or otherwise, without express written permission of the publisher.

FIND THE FIRST SOUND 'B'

1

Circle the objects that begin with the 'b' sound.

'B' AS IN BALL

FIND THE FIRST SOUND SOFT 'C'

2

Circle the objects that begin with the soft 'c' sound.

'C' AS IN CINEMA

FIND THE FIRST SOUND 'HARD C'

3

Circle the objects that begin with the hard 'c' sound.

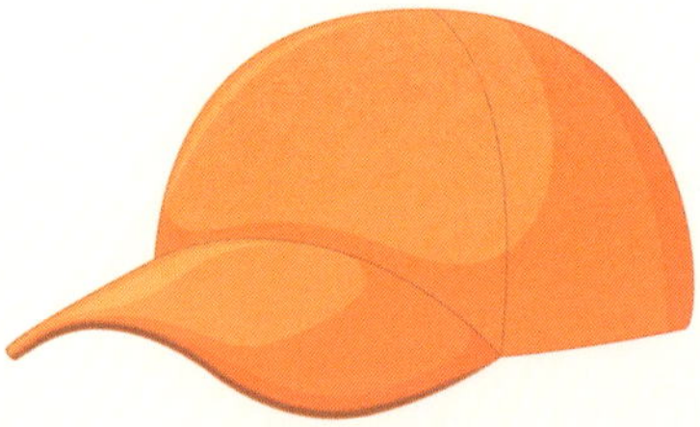

'C' AS IN CAT

FIND THE FIRST SOUND 'D'

4

Circle the objects that begin with the 'd' sound.

'D' AS IN DUCK

FIND THE FIRST SOUND 'F'

5

Circle the objects that begin with the 'f' sound.

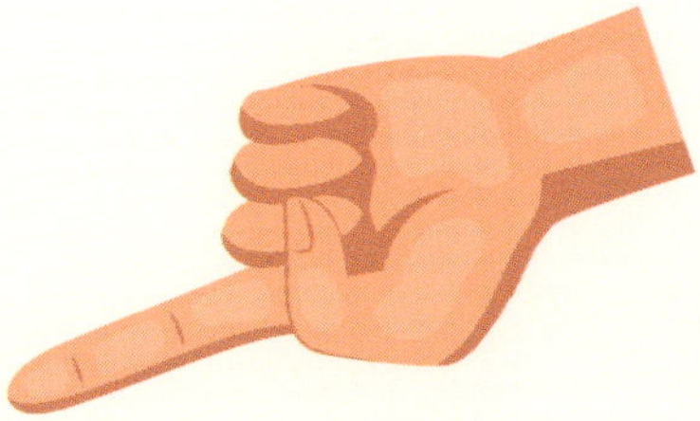

'F' AS IN FLOWER

FIND THE FIRST SOUND 'SOFT G'

6

Circle the objects that begin with the soft 'g' sound.

'G' AS IN GEM

FIND THE FIRST SOUND HARD 'G'

7

Circle the objects that begin with the hard 'g' sound.

'G' AS IN GOAT

FIND THE FIRST SOUND 'H'

8

Circle the objects that begin with the 'h' sound.

'H' AS IN HAT

FIND THE FIRST SOUND 'J'

9

Circle the objects that begin with the 'j' sound.

'J' AS IN JAM

FIND THE FIRST SOUND 'K'

10

Circle the objects that begin with the 'k' sound.

'K' AS IN KETTLE

FIND THE FIRST SOUND 'L'

11

Circle the objects that begin with the 'l' sound.

'L' AS IN LEAF

FIND THE FIRST SOUND 'M'

12

Circle the objects that begin with the 'm' sound.

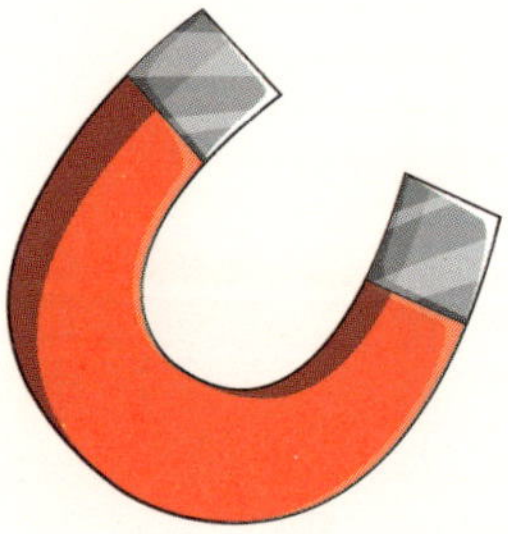

'M' AS IN MUG

FIND THE FIRST SOUND 'N'

13

Circle the objects that begin with the 'n' sound.

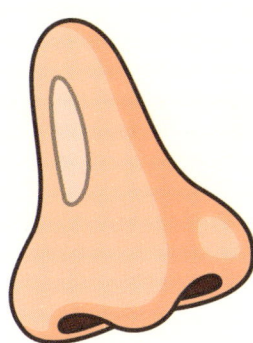

'N' AS IN NUT

FIND THE FIRST SOUND 'P'

14

Circle the objects that begin with the 'p' sound.

'P' AS IN PENCIL

FIND THE FIRST SOUND 'Q'

15

Circle the objects that begin with the 'q' sound.

'Q' AS IN QUILT

FIND THE FIRST SOUND 'R'

16

Circle the objects that begin with the 'r' sound.

'R' AS IN ROCKET

FIND THE FIRST SOUND 'S'

17

Circle the objects that begin with the 's' sound.

'S' AS IN SALT

FIND THE FIRST SOUND 'T'

18

Circle the objects that begin with the 't' sound.

'T' AS IN TOP

FIND THE FIRST SOUND 'V'

19

Circle the objects that begin with the 'v' sound.

'V' AS IN VASE

FIND THE FIRST SOUND 'W'

20

Circle the objects that begin with the 'w' sound.

'W' AS IN WORM

FIND THE FIRST SOUND 'B'

21

Circle the objects that begin with the 'x' sound.

'X' AS IN X-MAS

FIND THE FIRST SOUND 'Y'

22

Circle the objects that begin with the 'y' sound.

'Y' AS IN YOGA

FIND THE FIRST SOUND 'Z'

23

Circle the objects that begin with the 'z' sound.

'Z' AS IN ZOO

SPOT THE BEGINNING SOUND

24

Circle the beginning sound of each object in the row and colour the correct letter.

SPOT THE BEGINNING SOUND

25

Circle the beginning sound of each object in the row and colour the correct letter.

SPOT THE BEGINNING SOUND

26

Circle the beginning sound of each object in the row and colour the correct letter.

SPOT THE BEGINNING SOUND

27

Circle the beginning sound of each object in the row and colour the correct letter.

SPOT THE BEGINNING SOUND

28

Circle the beginning sound of each object in the row and colour the correct letter.

SPOT THE BEGINNING SOUND

29

Circle the beginning sound of each object in the row and colour the correct letter.

_AK

G   Y   S

_ITY

B   L   C

_OPE

W   N   R

WHERE'S MY FIRST SOUND?

30

The first letter of each object is missing! Follow the maze to find the correct beginning sound.

_ANDWICH

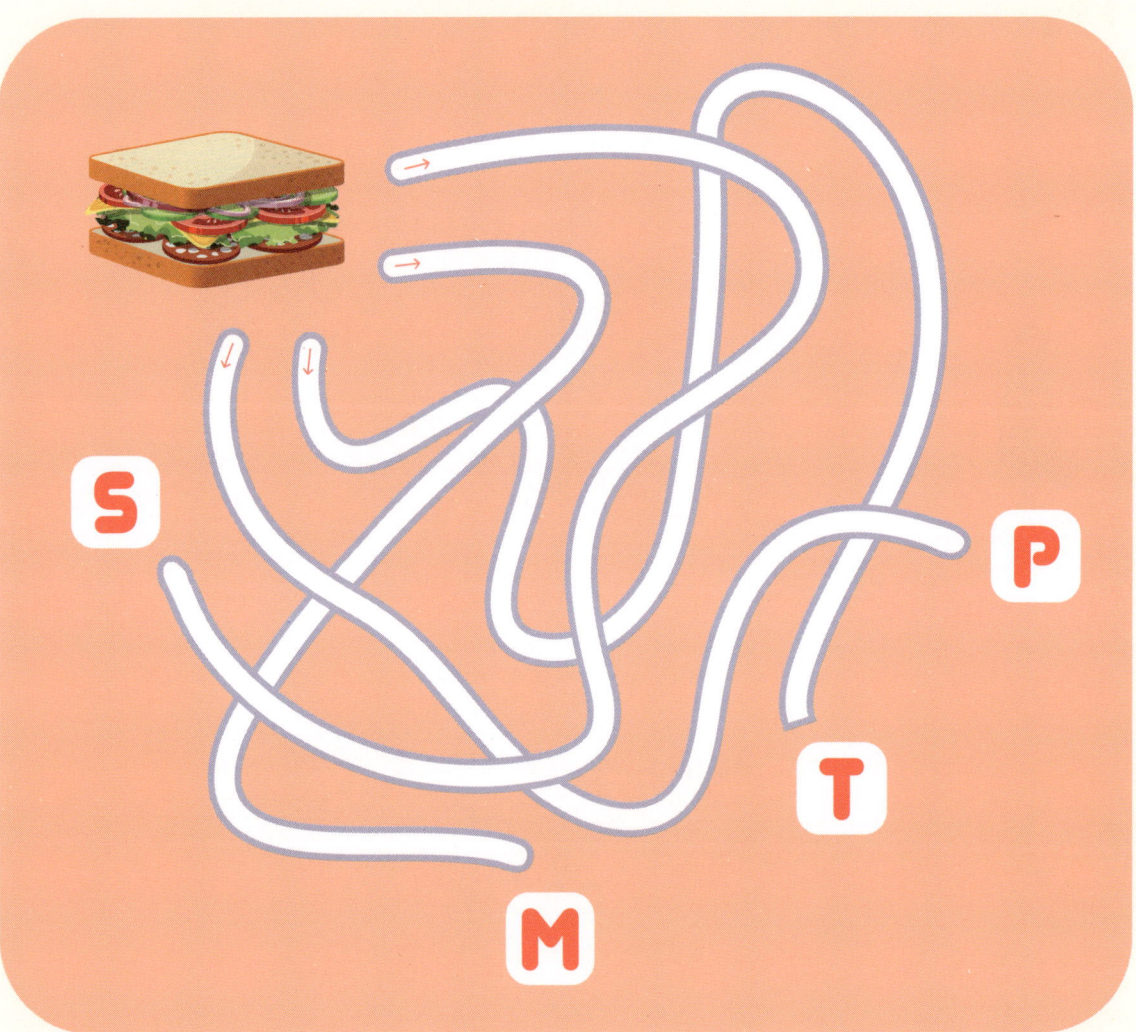

WHERE'S MY FIRST SOUND?

31

The first letter of each object is missing! Follow the maze to find the correct beginning sound.

_ARROT

WHERE'S MY FIRST SOUND?

32

The first letter of each object is missing! Follow the maze to find the correct beginning sound.

_OPCORN

WHERE'S MY FIRST SOUND?

33

The first letter of each object is missing! Follow the maze to find the correct beginning sound.

_OLPHIN

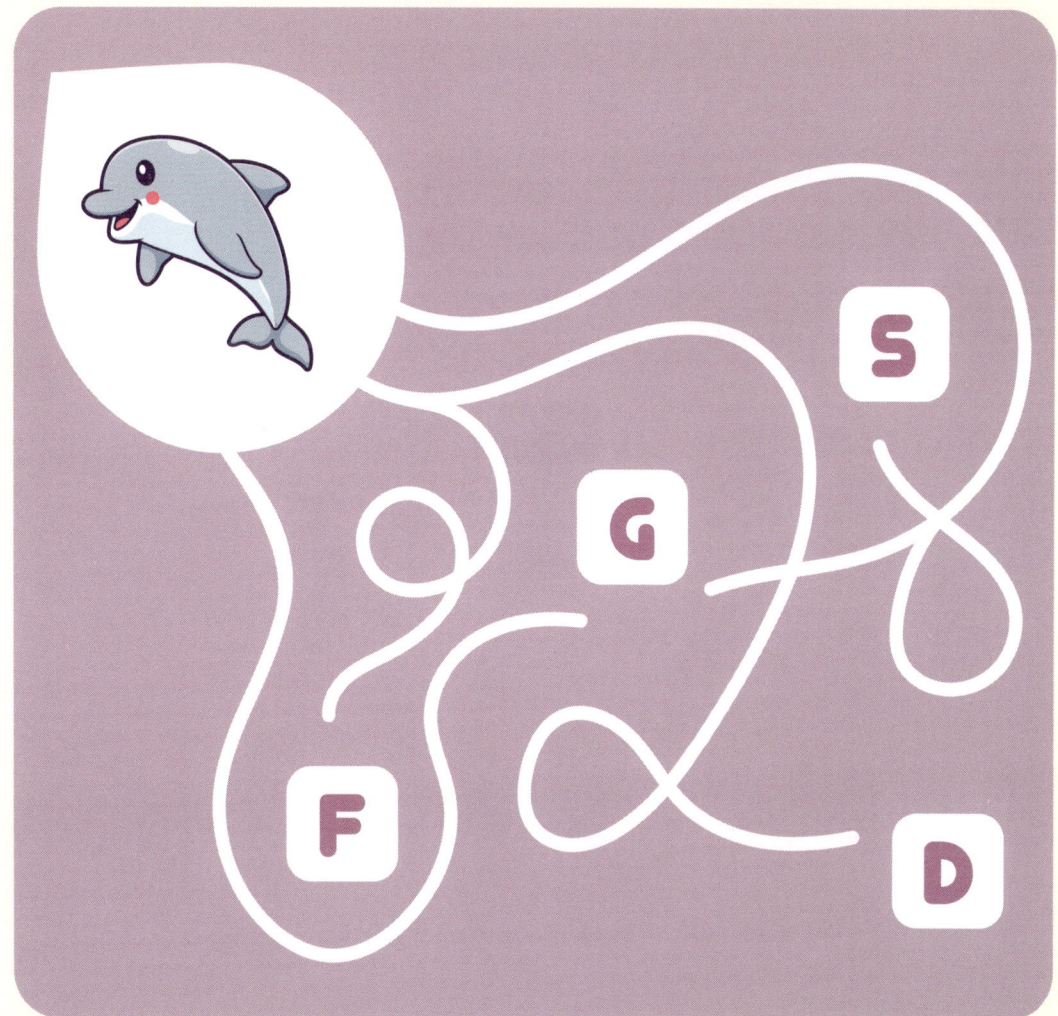

WHERE'S MY FIRST SOUND?

34

The first letter of each object is missing! Follow the maze to find the correct beginning sound.

_OBOT

WHERE'S MY FIRST SOUND?

35

The first letter of each object is missing! Follow the maze to find the correct beginning sound.

_UFFIN

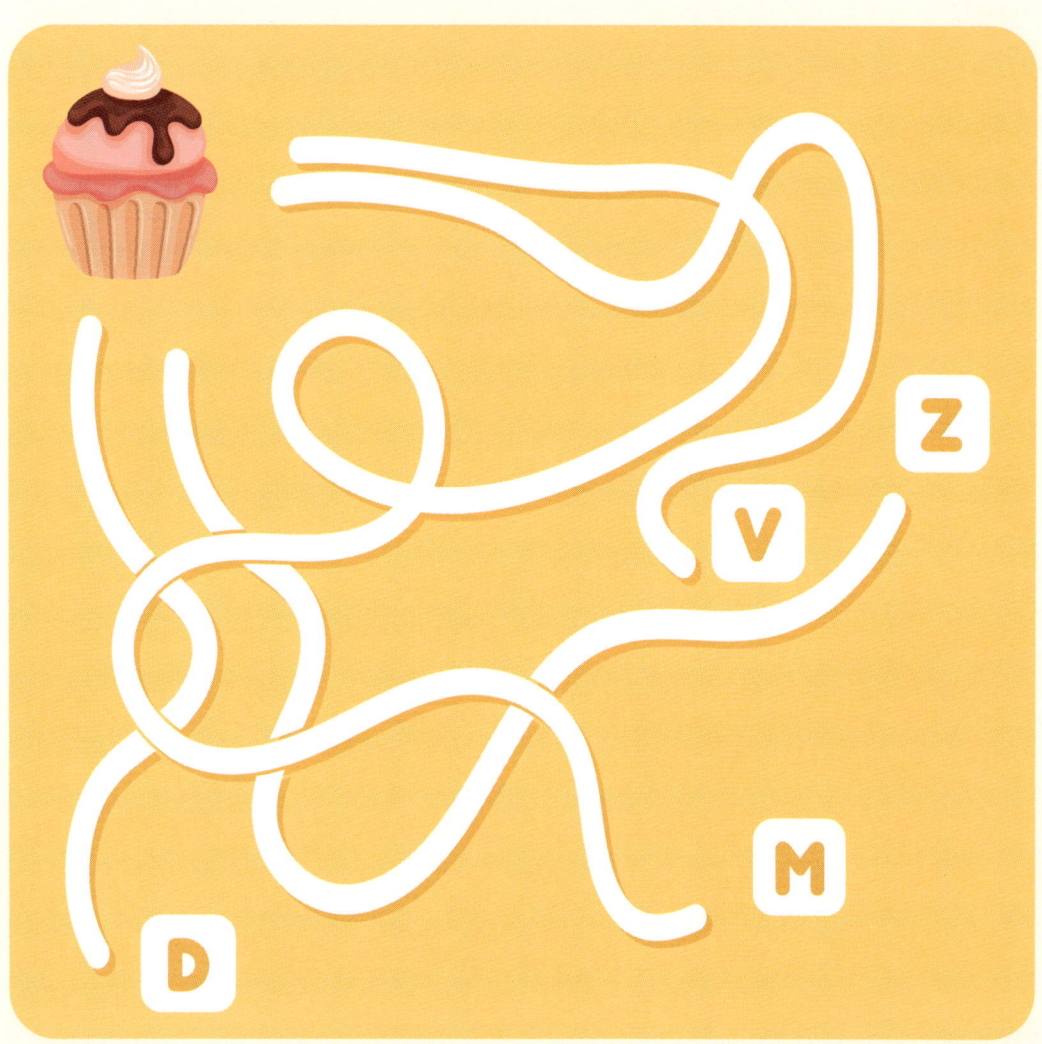

SORT BY SOUND: B AND C

36

Read the words below and sort them into the correct sound box—B or C.

'B' SOUND

....
....
....
....

B AS IN BALLOON

SOFT 'C' SOUND

....
....
....
....

C AS IN CELLPHONE

Bill
Cycle
Band
Saw
Circle
Bow
Sea
Celery
Steam
Bench
Cylinder
Stove

Note for parents: Read the words aloud and help your child sort them correctly.

SORT BY SOUND: C AND D

37

Read the words below and sort them into the correct sound box—C or D.

HARD 'C' SOUND

....
....
....
....

C AS IN CAMERA

'D' SOUND

....
....
....
....

D AS IN DICE

Cut
Thumb
Diary
Sail
Calm
Seed
Deep
Cart
Kite
Dance
Cold
Dots

Note for parents: Read the words aloud and help your child sort them correctly.

SORT BY SOUND: F AND G

38

Read the words below and sort them into the correct sound box—F or G.

'F' SOUND

F AS IN FACE

SOFT 'G' SOUND

G AS IN GIRAFFE

Fan
Phone
Gem
Fist
Jam
Giant
Fall
Photo
Gym
Feet
Kangaroo
Ginger

Note for parents: Read the words aloud and help your child sort them correctly.

SORT BY SOUND: G AND H

39

Read the words below and sort them into the correct sound box box—G or H.

HARD 'G' SOUND

....
....
....
....

G AS IN GOOSE

'H' SOUND

....
....
....
....

H AS IN HEART

Game
Van
Hit
Gold
Jug
Hand
Gum
Mug
Hop
Girl
Cap
Heat

Note for parents: Read the words aloud and help your child sort them correctly.

SORT BY SOUND: J AND K

40

Read the words below and sort them into the correct sound box—J or K.

'J' SOUND

....
....
....
....

J AS IN JET

'K' SOUND

....
....
....
....

K AS IN KIWI

Jump
Gift
Kitten
Jog
Cup
Kid
Just
Gems
Kite
Joke
Corn
Kit

Note for parents: Read the words aloud and help your child sort them correctly.

SORT BY SOUND: L AND M

41

Read the words below and sort them into the correct sound box—L or M.

'L' SOUND

....
....
....
....

L AS IN LEOPARD

'M' SOUND

....
....
....
....

M AS IN MIRROR

Lens
Nap
Mat
Lace
Blue
Mill
Lawn
Wand
More
Lip
Yellow
Map

Note for parents: Read the words aloud and help your child sort them correctly.

SORT BY SOUND: N AND P

42

Read the words below and sort them into the correct sound box—N or P.

'N' SOUND

....
....
....
....

N AS IN NOODLES

'P' SOUND

....
....
....
....

P AS IN POP-CORN

Nest
Knee
Pack
Name
Box
Pipe
Night
Knife
Purse
Nose
Bug
Page

Note for parents: Read the words aloud and help your child sort them correctly.

SORT BY SOUND: Q AND R

43

Read the words below and sort them into the correct sound box box—Q or R.

'Q' SOUND

....
....
....
....

Q AS IN QUEEN

'R' SOUND

....
....
....
....

R AS IN ROSE

Quiet
Cube
Read
Quail
Rail
Kite
Quack
Rust
Cucumber
Quick
Wrap
Round
Smile
Wrist

Note for parents: Read the words aloud and help your child sort them correctly.

SORT BY SOUND: S AND T

44

Read the words below and sort them into the correct sound box box—S or T.

'S' SOUND

....
....
....
....

S AS IN SOUP

'T' SOUND

....
....
....
....

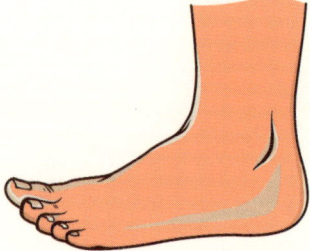

T AS IN TOES

Sail
Circle
Tap
Sew
Drum
Tick
Sand
City
Toast
Sell
Dry
Time

Note for parents: Read the words aloud and help your child sort them correctly.

SORT BY SOUND: V AND W

45

Read the words below and sort them into the correct sound box—V or W.

'V' SOUND

....
....
....
....

V AS IN VEGETABLES

'W' SOUND

....
....
....
....

W AS IN WHISTLE

Vase
Tea
Wear
Valley
Van
Wide
Voice
Wand
Wave
Vet
Smile
Word

Note for parents: Read the words aloud and help your child sort them correctly.

SORT BY SOUND: X, Y AND Z

46

Read the words below and sort them into the correct sound box—X, Y or Z.

'X' SOUND

....
....
....
....

X AS IN X-MAS

'Y' SOUND

....
....
....
....

Y AS IN YELLOW

'Z' SOUND

....
....
....
....

Z AS IN ZOO

Xylophone
Van
Yam
Zebra
X-ray
Yell
White
Zip
Yarn
Zap
Wand
Yolk
Smile
Zoom

Note for parents: Read the words aloud and help your child sort them correctly.